Let

Timothy Liu

saturnalia books

Distributed by Independent Publishers Group
Chicago

Let It Ride

Timothy Liu

Saturnalia Books
105 Woodside Rd.
Ardmore, PA 19003
info@saturnaliabooks.com

ISBN: 978-1-947817-08-1
Library of Congress Control Number: 2019937973

Book Design by Robin Vuchnich
Printing by Versa Press

Distributed by:
Independent Publishing Group
814 N. Franklin St.
Chicago, IL 60610
800-888-4741

The poems in this book first appeared in the following publications: *American Journal of Poetry, Ampersand Review, Boston Review, Boulevard, Brooklyn Rail, Caliban, Columbia: A Journal of Literature & Art, Columbia Poetry Review, The Common, Field: Contemporary Poetry and Poetics, Gulf Coast, Interim, Lana Turner, Literary Matters, Loose Change, Los Angeles Review, Mandorla: New Writing from the Americas, Matter Monthly, Michigan Quarterly Review, New England Review, New Orleans Review, Ocean State Review, Ping-Pong, Plume, Poetry Crush, Prairie Schooner, Prelude, The Progressive, Psychology Tomorrow, Rattle, Salmagundi, South Florida Poetry Journal, Souvenir, Superstition Review, Talisman, Tin House* & *Truck*.

Special thanks to Brian Henry, Joe Hall, Henry Israeli, Matthew Shelton, Brian Tierny, Luke Johnson, Rob Ostrom, and Chris Salerno for helping me divide the wheat from the chaff.

do Mhaitiú

thar teanga

Table of Contents

See, see rider.

See what you done done.

Lawd, Lawd, Lawd.

CURRENCY

It was in between all seasons I had known.

The bottoms of my soles worn flat.

What else to conceal?

The restaurant check came back.

A dollar less each time.

He who paid me twice what anyone's worth.

Till I was eating off of him for free.

His tongue all coin.

His mattress stuffed with specie.

Spindled regrets.

Sending me downriver on his makeshift raft.

LET IT RIDE

The cards left on the table edged with gilt.

I'm all in, he said, so long as you respect complicity.

Now you see it, now you don't.

As if language could be trusted one iota less.

No is sexy! blurted out at the end of every billable hour.

An exit mistaken for an entrance.

So much we did not say.

Between the gesture and the act.

Between his legs of a sudden my privacy breached.

A pint of the black stuff at McDaid's.

A drop of Writer's Tears.

Our wives in some back room raising the stakes.

ON MARRIAGE EQUALITY

They don't do couples counseling.
They go to Home Depot, they go to Lowe's,
figure out what it would cost
to tear their kitchen out, replace
the granite counter tops, the stainless
steel, that was so last year.
They think the market is strong.
They take out home equity loans.
They take their "date nights" seriously,
scheduling in "quality time" and faithfully
meeting their mutually agreed upon
weekly coitus quota.
They do Pilates, they do Bikram yoga.
They enroll in "positive" Tantric sex workshops
and swing with other couples
who "sing the body electric."
They post romantic kisses on Facebook,
tweet about lubricants and lingerie,
put tally marks on a white-erase board
for the number of times they've come
each week, their little wink wink
(unless friends ask, don't tell).
She knows his passwords, reads his emails,
closely watches his history cache, careful
not to delete the cookies.
Is his cock really big enough?
Can he tell she's faking it, her intensity
just a little forced, this woman
who knows how to back into a parking space
with her eyes closed, who can talk her way

out of any moving violation?
He says he's not a misogynist, gives
plenty to Planned Parenthood,
says he'd keep on doing it
even if it weren't a tax write off.
He keeps his fingernails trimmed.
He keeps an underage boy
in a soundproof room walled-off with foam.
She wears Lanvin, Louboutin.
How much longer can this go on?

SILVER ANNIVERSARY ODE

My husband breaks his back
molar on a piece of gravel

stuck in a bowl of rice

and beans I cooked for him
before retiring to bed,

wanting him

to have something after spending
a late night at the office

preparing a legal draft

to cover his own ass with HR
when a more-than-competent

underling has consistently shown up

less than half the days he's paid
to work, and I won't go

into all the details

nor will I mention how it has
crossed my mind that either of them

could be having an affair

if anyone would bother
to ask, which I don't, and it

looks like the tooth will cost $650

to repair which is more than
twice what it will cost

to replace the forty inch

flat screen our cat knocked over
when workers started

jackhammering the sidewalk

two floors below and freaking kitty
the fuck out, a 4K smart TV

we only got to watch

one episode of Westworld on
before dragging the thing

down to the basement
where everything we no longer want

magically disappears, and this

my friends is what it feels
like to be married over 25 years,

our collective libido

having trickled down to a stream
so thin the chances of it

making it all the way

to the storm drain
are less than half the time it'd take

for a five year old

to fold this poem into a plane
and fly it over a gorge

somewhere outside of Ithaca

where the void awaits,
where the suicides continue to leap

every chance they get.

LOVE POEM IN A STEAM ROOM

Hard to commit
to memory—their knees

brushing up against

my own as we recited
lines no one knew

by heart—our nostrils

singed—burnt scent
of eucalyptus as we got on

with the business

at hand not to be found
in any book of verse.

AS FAR AS CHO FU SA

I don't remember where
we were headed in

the dark, only the sound

of a forceful stream
of piss hitting the forest

floor when he stepped

away from me and right
then and there I knew

we had nowhere

to get to—our arrival
sounding all around

in a dark so dark

I couldn't see my hand
in front of my face

or anything else

put there—only his
insistence, an unimpeded

flow—and it seemed

my ears were made
for this, for I was his

audience and his

alone in that stillness
where even if a tree fell . . .

FALSE HEMLOCK

Lay me down on top
of your Hummer

like an 8-foot Douglas

spruce you hacked
down at the tree farm

on your way home

from a rest-stop
rendezvous—smell

of pine sap stuck

on hands that know
a thing or two about

how to swing an axe.

ROMANCE IN A RED STATE

Said he was a card-carrying
Tea Party member, asked

politely what I was after

the bedroom doors closed
and I said I was proud

to be another non-essential

government employee on
furlough—only wanting

to get the fucking job done.

ANTEDILUVIAN

Such tabloid frenzy once word got out.

Never mind the flood.

Consequences standing in for God.

Question lyric authenticity.

This need we have to rescue ourselves.

As thousands storm the stage.

To trust mistrust instead of money.

Please go on. And on.

Sun and rain and the in-between.

A media circus in his pants.

Aboard an ark of our own making.

Far easier to go than not.

And love you long as the moment lasts.

LOVE LETTER: FRENCH QUARTER

Two pigeons on my porch
inching closer—necks
ringed violet and green
in a Mardi-Gras iridescence.
Dirty squabs. Bullying
a sparrow away from the crumbs
I toss—post-Katrina
sirens drowning out
the St. Louis Cathedral bells
whose tones caress not one but two
plaster touchdown Jesuses
anchoring their respective lawns
no tourist dare walk upon,
not on a day like today.
Who wouldn't want to be
manicured like them
when the magnolias start
throwing down their blooms
in a shower of wilted
shoehorn splatter—the whole day
stained by the heavy scent
of honeysuckle wreathing the air
with its seasonal jazz—
makeshift hucksters
sauntering through alleys
looking for a handout
I don't have, only a glance
of sweet malaise, my sawdust
throat humming a tune
that has no name.

BLIND WILLIE

For a beating that he gave
his woman for cheating
on him, she in turn threw

lye into his son's face
who'd just begun playing
a cigar-box guitar at the age

of seven—a tin cup strung
around his neck as he
learned to master regular

chords and open D for slide—
his future as a preacher
preserved in a gruff voice

shaking with fierce vibrato
pressed into a stack of
78s—a race-records

artist on the Columbia label
whose second release
was "Dark Was the Night"

and "It's Nobody's Fault
But Mine." Forget the father:
it's all about abysmal shouts

and groans that only a son
could make—an unidentified
female singer joining him

at a session in New Orleans—
his house later gutted by fire
as he slept in the charred

dampness of old newspapers,
never again to sing "Jesus
Make Up My Dying Bed"—

Chuck Berry, Beethoven
and Willie aboard the Voyager
sailing through outer space.

MEET ME UNDER THE WHALE

I don't remember what hour
it was we met, only that

the room was hot. I don't

remember if there was even
a clock in the room, only

that you had stolen the hands

off its face, eyes already
darting under the table—slips

of the tongue like paper cuts

we would get to suck on
while a chanteuse nonchalantly

took the stage. You looked

at me like a worm crawling
on a glass globe, waiting

for something to come along

and pluck you off. Seems
like we'd been ordering

off the same menus for years

only the prices had changed—
note for note, the songs

no longer recognizable

as we rode into the mouth
of a whale full of untold

myths, staircases spiraling

down. It hardly matters now
who asked for the check

or even who paid, how much

everyone got tipped. We
were in there for a long time

trying to decide—Master

the Tempest is Raging
tinged with its laissez-faire

jazz while our lady leaned on

a baby grand, her combs
inlaid with mother of pearl

thrown down—bleached bones

and tongues of the damned
washing up on shore

in the corners of our eyes.

CAPTAIN, O MY CAPTAIN

My inner preacher dropping slack-
jawed drawers till pigeon splatter
dislodged itself from the hayloft of

my mouth, landlocked, tongue-tied,
lollygagged, the cathedral dark
of my sawdust throat coated with

father of pearl where flypaper
möbius strips twirled pirouettes
through amnesiac stalls rimmed

by rosy dawn. Who wouldn't barter
away a lifetime of regret for a salt-
wet afternoon churning on the high

seas? His ball-busting cluster fuck
sent as anonymous text, my guard
towers taken down in that post-

storm deluge of surge-protected
codes, passwords and user names,
a versatile top looking to nail eight-

point bucks into a wall as he worked
his wiggly deep into my man-cunt—
my resistance broken by an easy

pinky. Count your many blessings
name them one by one and blah blah
blah blah blah see what God has

done! His Till-death-do-us-part
finger. His Fuck-you finger. His
Hey-I'm-number-one finger. His

Gee-look-at-my-thumb-it's-stuck-
inside-your-bum finger when he
saddles up and rides my ass out of

town, swaying underneath those
dusty Jerusalem palms, his wedding
band caked with shit, a Yom Kippur

without Leviticus, my dowry soaking
up sun in the Caymans for lack of
money does more to kill love than all

of the Pentateuch recited by rote,
the great religions of the world trying
to "tie or bind again" what time

relentlessly jostles loose. Forget
about God and look at me the way
you would a Rauschenberg when all

the guards are turning the other way.
I was meant to be touched, to fall
apart, not to be preserved for those

who'll never know what it was like
to have your dick in my mouth, yes
Sir!—sloppy and wet—mopping

up the scupper holes from fore to aft.

POEM

Beached on an alien shore, they

cut deep into his dolphin skin, started
in on removing the blubber

that cradled a full-grown man within—

hair still slick as if newly born
but dead already. No one really knew

what they were doing. *Let him live*

in two worlds, I said, *seal up*
his wound—there are no babies inside

his body, nothing there to harvest—

THE UNSAID

Drew his face on a sidewalk,
not with chalk but with

my mouth, my lips moist
against the hot cement

where girls had been playing
hopscotch all afternoon

until they were called in—

street lamps flickering on
in suburbs shielded

from the stars. He taught me
names for constellations

hard to forget—secret
passwords left on my body

the neighbors can't hose off.

GOING POSTAL

So you wanted me
to step down
from my pedestal,

not storm the mall
with my AR-15
water pistol the color

of a late daffodil
unsheathing itself
on a grassy knoll

in a child's drawing
affixed by magnets
to some motherfucker's

Frigidaire, is that
what sobriety has
come to? The vote

is sure to be split
5-4, you can count
on that, your stash

of airline bottles
smuggled out of first
class stumbled on

by a general brigadier
in search of a party
everyone wants to

crash. Even so,
I love how attentive
the strippers are

as they refill my glass
with water imported
from a spring no one

has ever travelled to,
not for all the tea
in the Dakotas. Tell me

when's the last time
a philatelist looked
this good on his knees

licking an upside-
down double-winged
Curtiss Jenny, knowing

full well the love letter
it was carrying wasn't
worth his own spit.

HIGH CHURCH

notes lodged inside a second-hand
instrument stripping his sound of all

vibrato he left behind like school

to earn a reputation   the Victrola
introduced in 1901 to respectable

homes where pianos would be soon

abandoned for shim-sham shimmies
as cane-chopping cotton-picking fads

danced their way across America

the Texas Tommy   the Turkey Trot
farmed to kids who couldn't read

but could be taught in the modest

elegance of an outhouse   primitive
provocative   his duty to reveal

to a world that would call him King

the highest and lowest   blowing
so hard the mute flew out of his horn

HIS LEGACY

but a voice blowing away the dust
on our daily lives   same songs   forced
into surrender well beyond
all spirituals   and minstrel tunes
sounding itinerant syncopations
in an age of decadence   no rue   nor gumbo
simple as that   what pains us must be
turned into gospel   swing
the angel and the devil separate but equal
underground   where the voices are
for if a trumpet can   why a trombone can too
no name at dawn but ragtime's birthed
amalgam on American soil
sounding its big noise   credit due
where lips to ecstatic blows
had gotten their lilt as a moan went through
you   high church   smoking
on a hotbed   till the night wore all of us
out   the missed gigs   flat notes
going flatter in the filtered light
where folklore colossi were playing for whores
on scandal sheets   spindled pages
of dime-store novels wafting in
the perfume of his life   his legendary
voice   in which no recordings   survived

I LOVE MY WIFE

He puts his hands
on my knees and says
"I love my wife!"

He orders Dom Perignon

and baked foie gras,
filet mignon and flaming
cherries jubilee, asks me

to strike the match.

The waiter asks if that
will be all, clearing away
the plates as my lover

signs the check, looking

me straight in the eyes
and saying: "I love
my wife!" He grabs

the rubber ring, pulls

the condom off the tip
of his cock after pulling
out of me and says

"Baby, I've got to go,"

leaving me to wonder
what he says to his wife
each night in their bed

when the lights go out.

ARE WE THERE YET?

He held his anxiety close
like a goldfish in a plastic baggie
leaking through his coat his cell
phone down to 20% how many folks
did he fuck over in the overhead
bunk of a tractor-trailer you wonder
as a ham-radio-operator shaves
the hair around your anal valve
my aerodynamic angel casting halos
into the air as if I were a Coke bottle
standing tall at the local carnival
those rubber rings out of reach
but for the barker's voice egging me on
to give it another try my cock
poking out of a fag hag's knock-off bag
a Louis Vuitton without the tags
if only he could accept my mother
jacking off the neighbor's dog he too
would lay off on the sauce and commit
all 12 steps to his shrink at once
think nothing of those cotton-candy
colored sheep leaping over from
this world into a dozen traffic lights
burning red down the boulevard why not
go ahead and grab the bull running
rampant through a china shop
made in China, ass-burger murder
on the rise over billions served
my Alabaman stuck in Newtown again
without a protein bar or a bottle

of water from a virgin spring it's time
to clear the decks sail on through
military bed sheets tucked and cornered
with all-night farts & armored cars
slipping gears—our crank-shaft gasket-
blown treasure trove bottomed out.

HE HELD

his sadness

close to his chest
like a breadbox

that concealed a violin

too small for even
a child's hands

to play—

LET IT RIDE

He eyes a box of ammo when I
put my hand on his fly, ready

to take me out. What the fuck

were we doing in a time share
neither of us belonged to,

having hopped a security fence,

having left our fingerprints
on sliding glass, the leaf-choked

pool needing some care it clearly

wasn't going to get—his hands
grabbing the back of my head

like a bowling ball a child holds

for the very first time, trying to
avoid the gutters when no one's

counting spares—a jockstrap

stuffed down my throat. Might've
found love if the horse trough

wasn't sloshing piss with wasted

pickup lines—my auctioned Ken
and Barbie Van worth more

had we kept the original box.

TRUE VALUE

Why not destroy the thing you
love most? Like the mouse
stuck on a glue trap held

under water till the bubbles
rising from its mouth stopped
breaking on the surface

and you knew everyone in
the house would get some sleep
but you. Like the comic book

collection in a garbage can
your father doused with
gasoline and torched one

afternoon after church when
he wanted to show you how
much he loved his own god

more than you. Thirty years
later, you'd stay up late
at night, recollecting what

you exactly lost, searching
on eBay for every issue
of every title in its last known

condition, but no matter how
hard you tried, something
escaped you, some nuance

floating away on newsprint
cinders caught in a breeze
before settling back on a lawn

still waiting for you to mow
on any other day but Sunday.
You got on your bike and rode

to the corner five and dime
but never spun the rack again
with Marvel super heroes

gazing out at you. Like eyes
of mice with faces stuck
to the black tar, whiskers

twitching to those squeals
echoing off a kitchen floor
that would disturb your sleep

for years to come—the Raft
of the Medusa some artist
painted arresting your own

eye as you sauntered down
a gallery on another continent
a lifetime after any of this

actually happened. Gericault
was the name you'd later
recall while perusing a beat-up

monograph sent Express Mail
by someone who bothered to
spend more on metered postage

than your father did on your
entire comic book collection—
a father who let those demons

he called "Legion" loose as he
preached to you from scriptures
marked in red. The same father

who later sent a second-edition
Random House unabridged
dictionary for your twenty-first

birthday after asking you what
you wanted, tossing in a copy
of *Kind of Blue* which would

linger for years on your shelves
collecting dust. You can walk
past a painting a hundred times

and never stop to take it in,
then one day, you're thumbing
through a gift sent by someone

you adore, and you have to
work hard to keep your tears
from splashing on a godforsaken

raft. Or you can find yourself
kneeling in an aisle of a True
Value where mousetraps hang—

where the eyes of super heroes
gaze out at you and this sudden
urge to drown them in a tub filled

with gasoline comes over you
as you flick the wheel of a lighter—
quickly turning pages of a book

you'll never want to read again.

THE FAMOUS POET

at my party eyes
the shelves to see if his books

are there. Apparently

not. Stares. Wondering what
the fuck he's doing there.

AUTHENTICITY

caught up in a rhythm of speak-easy love

societal strictness as the grounds for drink

so found themselves exorcised of doubts

orthodoxy sabotaging the selfless selves

frolicking hard till the curtain came down

came in alone went out a stranger music

sounds more dog than dog would ever be

as praise embarrassed his gleaming horn

passersby rubbing fingers on his cheeks

to see indeed if the color would come off

IF GOD BE A WHITE MAN

then this must be
Bamboula—wild and unaccountable
against the eardrum's fluent
doggerel where trance-like voodoo
induced ecstatic states
supplicating to Dambella or Da—
serpent deities—our clothes torn off
pell-mell in the hot dense dark
with saints and angels
employing tones for which there are
no written notes—Gullah
song propelled by minstrel banjo riffs,
hip shakes, shimmies, shoulder
rolls in mazooka time
hurling boozed-up slurs in torrential
two-four ragtime onus
all the way from piano to voice—
the olio's jazzy centerpiece
in Main Street's usual honkytonks
full of low-life clientele
pioneering royalties for left-hand
oompahs intensified, sifted
into a broken lexicon
heard in gutbucket cabarets suffused
with quarter tones
and Irish cadences more free-
flowing than coon-shouting whites
in black face booking
studio time where ringside brass-band
ballyhoo prototyped instrumental
growls and smears
into a veritable *imitatrices de la voix*—

LAST CALL (FOR DIZZY G)

if you don't yet thirst

for the sweat beading
on my lip   darling

you've already

missed it   what's seen
is gone   the pennant

lost   pent-up rage spent

on pleasure's idle
dregs storming a stage

where the matinee

idol lingered   faceless
fans jitterbugging

the aisles   dreams

fired through the mind's
electric grid   trains

of thought uncoupling

our truest loves
never   contracted

for exacted labors

however devoted
or disturbed   drink

into the far-off

zenith   uncontested
scat loading down

your money bags

left at some hotel
you've never checked

into   your father's

famous fudge   packed
in Christmas tins

demanding nothing

less   than freedom
from the tyranny

of his unsung chords

DOUBLE TIME

a jazz
be-bop melody
could hardly unsex
Dizzy who blew
epistrophe out of the V.-
F.W. doors—syncopated bu-
galoo out-
harass-
ing ranger
joes smoking blues and BBQ—
kiss-ass crip-crap
lollygagging ho-
mo gang-banged fun
no greater than the sum
of their shameful
parts where crackerjack
queens all stupid on mary j
rollicked in the pews—ASCAP and BMI
sucked off and high
till kingdom came—gog magog
under house arrest if
vodka-shot scats were crime
wherever dosed
XXs marked the spot—high-C
yodels sailing all the way past hip-flab
zenana

LYRICAL TOURISM AS A FORM OF TERRORISM

Where in the world

can I go
where a suicide

bomber is least

likely to blow
us up is

what I'm thinking

while window shopping
for cheap fares

online while on

sabbatical. Just this
morning someone blew

themselves up behind

the Blue Mosque
near where I

believe I once

splurged on some
steam rising up

through a reticulated

dome carved out
of stone—daylight

filtering back through

in radiant beams
while a man

more than twice

my own weight
walked expertly along

my spine, cracking

me in places
I didn't know

I had, we

who never exchanged
a word, only

looks, hand gestures

issuing easy commands
even a child

could follow, dried

leaves and branches
whipping my back

clean, my piss

cloudy later on
when I stepped

back out into

the world utterly
dazed as I

roamed on through

the Spice Market,
not intending to

buy saffron imported

from Iraq until
I knew what

the going rate

was even when
I was repeatedly

told I was

the day's first
customer and had

earned myself preferential

treatment, would I
like a glass

of tea, Turkish

Delight stacked up
in a pyramid

on a silver

tray, and I
thought: why not,

what harm could

come to us
on a day

just like any other.

THE GREEN WALL

In Marrakech, the medina walls
stand nine cubits tall. Easy to miss
the poverty. Or the contentment
of a camel bellowing its low
gutturals on a clay trail winding
through the Ourika Valley,
a tourist saddled on his throne
led about by a boy who knows how
to work a rope, make the beast
kneel down on all fours. Forget
about the vats of pigeon shit
mixed with lime, the stinking hides
and piles of matted fur scraped off
by dye-stained hands that won't reach
fifty, your leather wallet fat
with dirhams. Don't resent having
to pay outsider rates, 300 dirhams
for a bottle of *huille d'argan*
at the Berber women's cooperative
instead of 60. Is it really fair
you come from a place teaching others
how to write whether they have
the gift, or no, an off-season break
the one chance you've got to prove if
you're a fake, the Souks full of clay
tagines and Berber bracelets made
in China, Vietnam, Thailand, wherever
labor's even cheaper. Had to fly
across six time zones in order to find
peace of mind—status updates

letting others know how good you are
at being alone, no snake charmers
to be found in the Jemmal Fna.
Whatever remains of your money
and time, let it ride on roulette.
Nurse your *lait aux dattes* by the pool.
Only up in the Atlas Mountains
where zero bars rule the skies
can you still find yourself trapped
inside a cab without a rearview mirror—
your phrasebook Arabic useless
when a tour bus rear-ends into you.

LOVE LETTER: MARRAKECH

He says, *Would you like to have a look*
inside? You're already pretty close
to broke, but why not, he doesn't need

to know. Most of the bracelets are made
by machine, designs stamped onto
sterling blanks. You know he'll take

his lighter to the embedded stones—lapis,
coral, hematite—to prove they aren't
fake. By now you've found yourself

far back enough of the store to feel
like getting lost, nor wanting to speak
as he leads you by the hand behind veils

of silk that hang down to your feet
to where the mint tea has been steeping.
Are you looking for something special

for your wife?, he asks, his arm brushing
yours as he pours the tea with flair
from shoulder height, the golden stream

filling the glasses more than half full
before he empties them back into the pot
only to pour again, the tea finding its

level there where your fingers touch
the glass, the sugar in the metal box
not cubes nor bricks but crystal chunks

as you reach into your pockets, pulling
out whatever change you've still got left—
who said anything about going home.

THE LAND OF NOD

Having exposed yourself to public scrutiny.

Pre-exilic prophetic figures.

Assets siphoned through escheatment.

Your candidacy rescinded.

Was it hourly pleasure did you in?

There's no free money.

Unless someone out there loves you enough—

THE CUSTODIANS OF BLISS

come out at night, indifferent
to the ground hog in my gut

playing dead, my password valid 24/7
if only I had a clue. The fear

escapes me, rummages through my things, crawling
under the sheets, underneath the river

of my husband's snores—makeshift raft
his body makes at 3 a.m. tossed and turned

awake by the churning of this animal
thing—helicopter S.W.A.T. team in its eyes

ready to take me out.

THE GREEN MOUNTAINS

I asked the footprints in the snow
if any of them belonged
to you, and the more I searched,
the more they began resembling

my own. Perhaps I was the one
who was lost—whiskey sours
lacing my breath, my stumbling
gait, and you out looking

for me like all those fathers
who were more than willing
to strip the shirts off their backs,
unbutton their trousers beneath

a full moon—their husky voices
answering each other's calls
as if all of them were born
with the same name. In this I was

wrong, for the one who had
the smaller foot, the shorter stride,
was the one I felt most sorry for—
the one out of breath, so busy

trying to cover everyone's tracks.

DISTURBED

It's true you did not expect to see your neighbor
shitting into the flowerpot where you had kept

the spare key for your lover, but there you were

looking out onto the fire escape just before dawn
when you knew you should have stayed in bed—

YOUR ABUSED INNER CHILD

led me to a hole, someone's eager
mouth, the tip of my cock wiped off
on the shirt tail of a stranger I'd never
meet again. No need to explain
why the Eiffel Tower gives me wood
and not the Empire State, why your neck
smells like the Boboli Gardens
while your cock smells like the Forum
in Rome after sundown when the bats
start circling, the food in the fridge
needing to be thrown out. My body broken
into. You who robbed me of feeling.
You who borrowed with no intention
of giving back any of my shirts, our bodies
the same size, take what you want I said
when what I meant to say was give me that
fucking shirt off your back, nothing fits me
anymore now that we've slept together,
now that you've peeled the labels off
my vodka bottles bobbing up and down
in a claw foot tub, and not a word
exchanged between us—only cum and
manly sweat—shirttails smuggled
out of a country that no longer exists.

ARS POETICA

It's not the smoking I miss
but his mouth reciting

verses in between taking

deep swigs. The water bottle
might have tipped me off

to his neediness. Who

needs to drink that much
throughout the day? Not even

a horse, and yes, some said

he was hung. Only thing worse
than a cobalt polystyrene

bottle ordered off Amazon

might be a flask of generic
vodka, the cheapest shit

sold at the nearest bodega

past midnight. Might want to
call it more than an oral

fixation sleeved in anonymous

paper wrap. Ever wonder
how many who manage

to finish a marathon

also happen to be in AA?
Nothing against rehab

but why is it so many

relapse? At ten grand a pop,
you might want to take it

more seriously. My godfather

who turned eighty finally
decided to get both of his

knees replaced. My brother

at fifty decided to get both
of his tubes untied, wanting to

start up another family.

How many times did I have to
watch someone breathing

through a hole in their throat

and speak to me directly
in that dehumanizing electric

voice during a commercial

break before I decided
I just had to disconnect

my cable, completely unplug

from the world grid? I'm not
better than any of you

but I do know one thing: a man

without a Soul Friend is like
a body without a head,

is like a polluted lake no good

for drinking. Darling, has it
come to this? Not that I want to

say goodbye to all the addicts

in my life, some of them wearing
masks that closely resemble

my own face. Camus said

you get to own your own face
around the age of thirty-five

and I remember finding that

a little upsetting. That was
more than fifteen years ago

and at fifty plus, I can tell you

what no one wants to hear:
that it's even more lonely

to be a head without a body

rolling around in a basket
at the height of the Revolution—

everyone else with heads on

shouting *Viva la France!*
I am still looking hard

for a Soul Friend, New York City

notwithstanding. Is it wrong
to want to believe in

Celtic wisdom handed down

through the centuries when I
identify as a gay ex-Mormon

Chinese-American swinger?

The Irish woman named Mary
who turned my cards over

wore a green polka dot cloak

and asked me what kind
of poetry I write, and when I

returned her volley with, well,

what kind do you read?, she
handed me a copy of O'Donohue's

Anam Cara. Today just happens

to be my Soul Friend's birthday.
Once again, we are the same

age, though he lives in Chicago

and no longer speaks to me.
He is like a body without a head,

I think, but what does he think,

our bodies still "commingled
in the well of dreams," not knowing

how we really lost our minds.

ROMANCE

Wanted to mention
how that bloody cut

of steak steaming

on your plate lurched
forward on its own

volition the moment

you looked away—
it was then I knew

what we were in for.

THE VIOLENCE

It was so quiet you could hear
an envelope being slid

under the door. Even without

tearing it open, you knew
it was over. The same way

you found an orange rind

that still had a whiff of citrus
to it and knew it was his

though he hadn't stepped

into your kitchen for years.
His hunger had been all

too casual, ear to your chest

late at night, the neighbor's
TV coming through the walls

with much excitement even if

the voices stayed muffled.
Back then you knew his cock

was the best thing between

you as he peeled off the shell
from your hard-boiled egg

morning after morning

in one complete spiral without
saying a word—the salt

on the table left untouched.

LET IT RIDE

He wanted sex without saliva,
sex without someone else's saliva
on his member, on his nipples
like his body was being marked
the way it dried on his skin—evidence
of someone else's desire
that would outlast his own need
to get fucked, to simply come,
knowing that when he came
or when the other man came
(whoever would come first)
the contract of the moment would be
fulfilled, and each would move on
to the next thing—another meal,
another man, whatever,
if only to rid oneself of the evidence,
yes, a stranger's saliva
already washing off under a faucet
in the nearest restroom he could find
as quickly as possible
to make his body clean again,
clean enough for the one
who was waiting at home
expressly to lick again with saliva
he wouldn't have to wash off,
could fall asleep to—the salivas
never mixing, never touching
the tongue of his wife,
to wash off the scent of a stranger
so the wife would never have to taste

and be woken from the dream
of their fidelity, the marriage vows
intact, this man who well knew
some things do not wash off
with antiseptic soap, this man who knew
there was a chance some things
had consequence, a taste, evidence
of an intractable illness already incubating
in its earliest stages even if
most likely not, a man gambling
with a future that wasn't just his own
however remote the chance—
not the cliché of lipstick on his collar—
he was too careful for that,
would erase all emails, the numbers
on his cell-phone bill blotted out
with permanent marker, hell, bills
that cried out to be shredded, and shirts
taken directly to the cleaners if not
outright incinerated—no dresses
left behind with presidential stains
on them as proof enough to stand up
in potential courts of law—
no, there'll be no fluids like that
to eat away at his dream, careless acids
only good for tabloid shame, a man
who knew how futile it was
to ask a stranger if he was "clean," if
his body was free of the plague
or some other such monument

the moment's pleasure sometimes makes
without being asked—
a stranger's saliva as messenger
whose secret message was written in codes
that only a medical test
could decrypt, a message immune
to antiseptic soaps—untold histories
that simply would not wash off
no matter how hard he scrubbed before
his companion came home
(a wife who had secrets of her own)
and what was a laptop's cache of porn
compared to this, for wasn't this
what he knew of love?—to take things
only so far, no farther—
so the two of them might live.

DE RERUM NATURA

The bliss wears off.

The blessed state comes to an end.

A snowflake melting down a windshield.

A windshield melting inside an atomic blast.

Everything dissolves.

A well-heeled fire burning in the hearth that freed our hands to tend one another.

Dawn heralding our last day, thermostat set at sixty.

All weekend the cottage was cold, winter dissolving into spring, the thaw just getting going.

In our post-coital haze, the universe seemed an even colder place.

His body covered with an alpaca blanket hand-woven in Peru, the backyard bonfire burning low on a bed of slow coals.

His wife and son in another city hundreds of miles away.

Me leaning down to kiss his cock that had shriveled into a bud.

To taste the last wetness.

All day I carried his seed inside me, my body lit from within.

Not like a Giotto angel.

Stronger than that, more raw.

Like a woodpecker spearing grubs in a lightning-struck pine, knocking hammered echoes through the woods.

Our minds attuned to sound alone.

To quickening breaths.

One likeness leading to another.

A vodka flask in a glove box drained to the dregs.

A face in a bathroom mirror looking like a preacher who will leave his congregation.

As the hours grow heavier, more fragrant, the mercury rising up to seventy.

All those years, desiring and resisting, resisting and desiring, he says!

What world are we even walking in?

A cardinal flits by in a blaze of color looking for his mate.

The welcome crash.

Song by song, bird by bird, soon to be buried under the sky's open vault.

THE BELOVED

who was among us has entered
the invisible   you must not
follow too closely   not at first
shards of porcelain on the floor
when you   lost it   having gone
too far   dusting the limoges
someone said it wasn't necessary
to rub your nose in the corpse
before it's tossed   the cremains
scattered   group burial refused
for you who never much liked
others   content now just to be
rid of the stench   pre-dawn yowls
filling up the house from under
the couch   a scent remains   rise
and explain   the alimentary canal
one tried to regulate   could not
towels and blankets hauled down
to the laundry room   tidiness
for days after as a means to bargain
the losses down   mechanically
you clean   the walk-in closets
baseboards   wherever the animal
hid   back and forth   a ghost
made visible   the new steps
you took   to choreograph grief

THE GIFT

The joint must have come a long way
to be with us, hints of oregano
smelling of skunk. Didn't you tuck it
in your sock as you sauntered
through the airport security check?
Neither of us even sure we were high.
Last night, my cat came back to me
in a dream, her coat a darker shade,
still bony in the way she had become
in her last days—one shot from the vet
and she was out, two shots and her heart
just stopped. Still dreaming, I said
to her, *but I know you're dead!*
Even my own dream couldn't fool me,
heavy sobs stirring me from sleep,
a half-smoked joint left somewhere
in your room. Last night you said,
smoke as much as you want, and I
knew you'd meant it, the joint having
traveled far to be with us, no farther.

DEAD-BEAT ODE

I am his

laundry service,
one he calls

when he's feeling

dirty. He takes
no starch

nor bleach—

wants a gentle
agitation cycle

and someone

like a mommy
to clean up

after him so he

doesn't have to
face the world

in all its stinking

glory he knows
he can't help

but keep on

consuming, a man
who at times

forgets how to

wipe his own ass
when falling down

drunk. Have you

seen him? Are you
the kind drawn

to this particular

type—the infant
slumped over

in a high chair,

baby bottle filled
with top-shelf

booze because

mommy simply
buys the best

or nothing at all.

ARS POETICA: AT FIFTY

Between two men
drinking from the same

glass, a choice

that often goes
unexpressed—green

olives passed back

and forth in the mouths
of a father and son

in a corner booth

where cock and regrets
have never spoken

openly about what is

most desired, a moment
spreading its rash

longings deep enough

where no one can
touch, soothe, or work

out all the tension

balled-up into knots—
yoga and mindfulness

on a mat drenched

with sweat unable to
compensate for faces

ramming up against

pubic bone where one
can still inhale

rising bread. The world

was wrong. Love allows
our tongues to follow

thirst to whatever needs

to be reached—a cube
of ice on a hot stove

riding its own melting.

AGAINST MYTH

Did we fly too

close to the sun,
its devouring

eye with blinders

full on, beads
of melting wax

loosening each

quill that kept
the whole show

going? It was

among other
things a father

and son story,

let no one tell
us otherwise—

Phaeton and his

pards no less
part of the same

sad tale. One

doesn't have to
read Ovid from

cover to cover

in order to know
how everything

will end. Or fly

by the seat
of our pants

in a drunken

stupor without
knowing where to

land, that much

is clear. Forget
about Williams'

poem about

Breughel's
painting—this

isn't that. Done

by the Elder
or the Younger

does it matter

to you? Do you
really want me

to bury you next

to your daddy's
grave in Wisco,

sprinkle a little

Skyy on the stone
bearing a name

you didn't get

to choose? Live
and let live is

not the same

as live and let
die. Let go

and let God is

not the same as
letting your darling

take the big car

out for a little
spin with no one

to watch out

where the story
can't help but

wanting to go.

PILGRIMAGE

No one knows when
Jeroen van Aken
was born—none
of his signed works
are dated although
there's proof he died
in 's-Hertogenbosch
in 1516 where he
seems to have spent
most of his life as
Hieronymus Bosch
and this is all
I have to go on
as I take my stroll
across Central Park
on a Sunday afternoon
in 2018 all the way
to Gallery 641
at the Met Museum
in order to adore his
Adoration of the Magi—
perhaps the only
real Bosch to be
spotted in this city—
angels with gold leaf
on their wings holding
up a green curtain
on a scene that looks
entirely staged—
Joseph hunched over,

barely able to
prop himself up
on a crutch, Mary
sleepy-eyed, no one
in the frame
(not even the Ox)
looking at the naked
flesh of an infant
standing straight up
in his mother's lap
with outspread arms
about to take flight
if god were a bird
building a nest
in the tower's exposed
crags rather than being
bound by gravity
like everyone else—
a tiny couple dancing
in the background
where rolling pastoral hills
are dotted with sheep
reminding us all
that we are nothing
more than a wayward
flock in search
of someone to gather us
in—the posed
tranquility of this scene
quite a disappointment

compared to what
Bosch is best
known for—angst-ridden
tableaus of the flesh
scorched and flayed
in the next gallery over
where a crowd
has gathered around a sign
mounted to the wall—
Christ's Descent
into Hell attributed
to a mere "follower
of Bosch" who for some
is as good as all
get out for unlike
Moses or Abraham,
at least we know
Bosch and his followers
lived!—that across
the Great Lawn
I can behold an actual
copy, and when security
happens to be turned
the other way, even touch
the two oak planks
grained horizontally,
held in place
with three dowels
near the center
of a panel exposed

in an X-radiograph—
earliest possible creation
date of 1491
indicated by
dendrochronological
analysis—its long lost
twin sequestered
in a private collection
in Milan—smoky
flames rising up
from the lower right
corner suggesting a fire
originally present
in the slightly less squarer
New York version
has been cropped
out—none of this visible
to the untrained eyes
of pilgrims for centuries
who happened by
this apparent fake
not to mention
how many times
it was packed up
and shipped off
to many distant cities
(Dallas, Iowa City,
Bloomington, Houston)
willing to pass it off
for the real thing

before I was born,
insensitive past
cleanings abrading
the delicate skin
of the uppermost
layers that render
this particular hell
more translucent
in the sky above
the ship's riggings
and that gaping mouth
impossible to ignore
as I behold
a group of teenagers
holding up their cellphones
to take selfies
of their pilgrimage
posted instantly
for the rest of the world
to like or comment
on—hardly matters
who or when
this thing was painted—
only that we're here.

HONEYMOON

My body is not
Afghanistan so perhaps

it's time you pull out.

TO AUTUMN

Harder to enjoy
the foliage this fall
when we hear reports
of folks scavenging
leaves off trees
to cook for dinner
in Eastern Aleppo
where the bakers
are cutting bags
of flour with bits
of dried spaghetti
ground up in order
to make a few extra
loaves they will sell
for $2.50 each
when the average
monthly salary now
for the families
that remain is less
than thirty dollars
and we wonder if
there's still something
we can do about it
in a republic where
elected officials
can't even correctly
name the country
this bombarded city
resides in, can't name
a single relief agency

we could donate to
if asked, the leaves
falling onto Central
Park's Great Lawn
holding us spellbound
even more than ruins
scattered throughout
the Met's Greek Wing—
damaged marble
whose colors time
has stripped away.

CARPE DIEM

You won't live

long enough to see
who will win the next

election, the blood

clot deep within
your artery breaking

free. You and I

won't make it to
those island dunes

we planned on

getting lost in—
all the money

gone. I tried

to tell you not to
worry about if

the per diem

would be enough
to cover everything

we had in mind.

I tried insisting
it was time for us

to splurge, go

ahead and come
on my chest!

I said, this is close

as we're going
to get to play now,

pay later. You

mumbled something
about desiring and

resisting, resisting

and desiring,
thanking me for

breaking the cycle,

your cum drying
on my face that I

refused to wash off

as we lay there
stunned, the TV on

with the sound off.

Forget about where
the remote ended

up. Forget about

how much room
service was going

to cost us after being

locked up for five
whole days, a do not

disturb sign hanging

on the other side
of a boutique hotel door

undisturbed. So what

if you ultimately
lost your kid or if I

lost my job. So what

if our carefully guarded
names were nothing more

than shit by the time

we walked out
of there smelling like

French-milled soap,

even sneaking out
an extra bar

from the undocumented

worker's cart when
she had turned a blind

eye. Forget about

leaving any kind of
decent tip when we

had clearly outstayed

our welcome.
Nor does it matter

whose name we chose

to register under,
smart enough to pay

cash, leave no paper

trail behind for
the resentment patrol

to find. If we had to

do it all over
again is not even

a question. Maybe

we were incredibly
selfish, stupid to

think we'd get away

with any of it,
smart phone discarded

under the bed

meaning one of us
would eventually have to

go back and answer

those messages
and texts that kept on

coming. Even you

would've agreed
things had gone on

for far too long.

BROMANCE

Try to remember
how the mouth

follows the hand

and not the other
way around,

didn't someone

teach you that
when you were still

willing to learn,

taste buds garlanding
the cathedral

of your mouth

as a heightened
warning system

to keep all harmful

substances at bay
to give you a chance

to learn something

about love?
There was a girl

from grade school

named Anne
who wanted me

to eat the chocolate

shake she managed
to concoct for me

under the wooden

lid of her desk
during recess

when everyone else

was outside
getting some sun

and fresh air,

not sure where
our teacher was

or if she thought

the two of us
would somehow find

trouble, the nurse

calling 911
for an ambulance

to get my stomach

pumped after
I had swallowed

nail polish. Anne

Hines was her name,
a fat unpopular

girl, the only girl

from second grade
whose name I still

remember. Skip

ahead five grades
to find me

on opening night

crying backstage
in the wings

of our production

of *Oklahoma!*
where I'd been cast

as an extra

doing barrel rolls
and side kicks

in a dance ensemble

number only I
had somehow lost

my nerve and a girl

who was also fat
and had a hairy

upper lip somehow

managed to
plant one right on

my mouth and you

could say I stopped
crying on the spot,

grossed out

this would be the way
I'd lose my virgin

lips to a girl

named Beth Anne
Infelice and had to

keep it a secret

all through high school,
even beyond. You

might wonder if

such traumas
could turn a kid

off. Or gay. I did

not ask for either
of their attentions

but that's exactly

what the universe
deemed to arrange

for me in the suburbs

of Almaden before
I even knew what

my dick was for—

two girls who probably
have no idea how

they made their names

indelible in the life
of a boy whose name

they won't remember.

I scan the same
class photos

yellowing behind

plastic sheets
whose adhesive

from those pages

have eaten into
the backs so deeply

you can't remove

the photos without
damaging the images

and so have to

leave them pretty
much as they are

decades later

after a few beers
chasing down shots

of top-shelf bourbon

with a straight man
you suspect might be

willing to listen

to your secret
woes, might be able

to bind those wounds

with salve issuing
from his own mouth

as he takes you

by the hand
and leads you on

to those places

where all the girls
you knew could not.

HAPPY TO HAVE TRAVELLED 3171 MILES FOR THIS

That day I basically ate the Full Fry
at Maggie Mays and little else, didn't

finish the soda bread—wasn't so dry

as it was heavy, fresh out of an oven
whose mortar you could brick a city with.

My phone said I'd taken 17,328

steps, climbed 5 flights. You do the math,
the metric conversions. Ever been on a date

with yourself? My Beloved back at home

raising a kid thousands of miles away
hadn't been here in years, and I alone

learning a language. His. Maggie Mays

emptying out. I could've stayed longer
but left with my thirst intact. My hunger.

Love Letter: Dublin

How was it

I'd hopped the pond
not downing a single pint

at the Guinness Distillery?—

the air thick
with a fat sweetness

like corn syrup hovering

over Cedar Rapids
while the bloke who asked

for a light

asked where I was from
then said "New Yorkers know

how to party

though from where you're from
Christmas lasts two days

when it's more like two weeks

over here," a fist
bump between us

and off he went

down cobblestones mostly wet
for my entire stay,

a thousand icicle lights

doubled in a puddle
growing at my feet

as I ashed my Cuban robusto

that cost too much
for whatever I did I did

to excess, a headless

torso on Grinder 86 feet away
messaging me as I made

my way through the hotel's

revolving door,
so I asked if he'd like to follow

upstairs, his clothes off

in an instant, a stranger
standing there

more responsive to my touch

than that tree in St. Stephen's Green
I laid my hands on

to see if Ireland had anything

to say to me, Henry Moore's
memorial to Yeats

looking haggard, beleaguered

from too many wars,
the covers on my queen-sized bed

thrown off for more nights

than I care to count—
the scones and clotted cream

from afternoon tea at Shelbourne's

making me sick to my stomach—
so many finger sandwiches

chased down with a brew

infused with bergamot—
the shower too hot

as he toweled off, crumbs left

on the mattress
as if I cared or needed to be

rid of him, sad

Nancy Wilson had died—
a duet with Cannonball Adderley

playing on my phone,

Bluetooth speaker abuzz
with "Save Your Love for Me"

blasted through paper-thin walls

when he asked how many more nights
would I be in town,

offering to take me

to the Powerscourt Gardens
if I could manage a DART to Bray

but I didn't know how

or said the wrong thing, unsaddled
at last on my last night

in Dublin, listening

to the hooves
of a well-hung horseman

passing by—

Also by Timothy Liu:

Vox Angelica
Burnt Offerings
Say Goodnight
Hard Evidence
Of Thee I Sing
For Dust Thou Art
Polytheogamy
Bending the Mind around the Dream's Blown Fuse
Don't Go Back To Sleep
Kingdom Come: A Fantasia
Luminous Debris: New & Selected Legerdemain (1992-2017)

Let It Ride was printed using the fonts Adobe Garamond Pro.

www.saturnaliabooks.org